November Quilt

Penelope Scambly Schott

A Publication of The Poetry Box®

Editing & Book Design by Shawn Aveningo Sanders.
Cover Design by Robert R. Sanders.

ISBN: 978-1-948461-16-0
Printed in the United States of America.

Published by The Poetry Box®, 2018
Beaverton, Oregon
ThePoetryBox.com

"Loneliness does not come from having no people around you, but from being unable to communicate the things that seem important to you."

~ C.G. Jung

November, 2017

✳ November 1 ✳

Maybe don't read this. You might get sad.
Or bored. Or pissed at how often I say *I*.

But sometimes I do say *you,* because you
are part of why I scribble. Please say *I get it.*

Shall we go on? They used to call me Penny.
A penny for your thoughts, as if nobody

ever said that before. They said it again.
A bad penny keeps turning up. All month

I'll be turning up like *pennies from heaven.*
Daily memo from my corner of the universe,

or else a crazy quilt of unmatched scraps.
Backing and batting. Batty, isn't it, stitching

notions into couplets? I offer you my fingers,
my messy mind, this pieced together quilt.

You, please be my smooth edging.

Did you mistake your parents for grown-ups?
I did. I believed each untruth they told me.

I also thought married people talked only
about boring stuff like calling the plumber.

I didn't see my father's vital body inside his suit
or my mother's softness. I suppose she knew

the construction workers were whistling at her —
not at eleven-year-old me, with my awkward

crab apple breasts I slouched to hide.
But I'd been hiding all along.

Was afraid of my parents. Hunched in terror.
What about you? Were you afraid too?

I remember each word I ever misspelled.
Two s's in *Miss Pell*. I studied new tricks

to survive, but the cliff edge felt so narrow.

✳ November 3 ✳

Let's address this page to physical fact.
She is a female bipedal mammal in good health.

She has mated and reproduced. Her hair is white
like her dog's hair, and nearly as unruly. She inhabits

the North American continent in the year 2017 A.D.
Or is it politically better to call it *The Christian Era*?

Beats me. I worry about such details. I mean, why
should Jesus determine what year I'm writing in?

It's the Jewish year 5778, the Chinese year 4715,
the Solar System 4.6 billion, give or take a few

million. But what's a million between you and me?
Let's talk Earth: I'm wearing two flannel shirts

and a wool shawl so as not to ruin the planet
by burning fossil fuel. No, I'm lying. When I'm alone,

I sometimes shove my thermostat to 74 degrees.

❈ November 4 ❈

Lives don't have plots; they have refrains.
Let's jump back to fifth grade in New York City

where the Russians would bomb first
because clearly we were much more important

than little Washington, D.C.. I sat with my spine
pressing the corridor wall, sorry to end my short life

next to fat Billy Fisher who smelled like burnt onions.
Hey, Billy, do you have to sit so close?

I still dream the goose-shit green walls of that hallway.
How in the burning world would I find my baby sister?

I had brought us both to school on the number 7 subway
and was in charge of bringing her home.

Last night in my dreams it was polar bears
tiptoeing ice cube to ice cube in warm Arctic seas.

Oh, my daughter, my daughter, barely making rent,
and my son with his twice-mended heart,

how can I save us all?

✳ November 5 ✳

When did you learn that even children can die?
A shocker, wasn't it?

Dying belonged to great-grandparents
with their same one question: *What grade are you in?*

The black and yellow metal Fall-out Shelter signs
dotted the sides of city buildings.

I imagined these secret clubs with beds and food
enough to save us all.

I discovered *The Diary of Anne Frank.*
All my life she has been my older sister.

I also tried to figure out Heaven but logistics
didn't compute. What if you married twice?

Which husband would you get? Or if you died as a kid,
would you still have birthdays in Heaven?

I was the smart big sister assuming I should know.
So I couldn't ask. Or didn't ask.

Maybe that's when I first felt lonely.

All these decades, and do I know my husband?
Sure, I claim he's predictable, but really,

inside that silence, what is he thinking about?
Computer chips or the universe? Or whether

he needs to go to the toilet? It's the same face
of deepest concentration. Our wordless dog

communicates more. Quick lick on the wrist
or wild shake of her ears. *Feed me, walk me,*

let me sleep on your pillow. Husband, partner,
bed mate, fellow creature, tell me who you are.

When we lie side by side in our plot on the hill
between wheatfields, it will be too late to ask.

What is your first memory of your mother's face?
Were you afraid of your father's temper?

When did you realize you had brothers? When
did you learn what a penis wants? Do you ever

despair? Or can you mostly distract yourself?
I ache to know but asking never works.

We sleep alone together. We are not twins.

How can anyone bear to watch the news?
Or even listen?

National Public Radio rattles on in the kitchen.
My husband eats cereal with walnuts and bananas.

He looks at cartoons on his laptop
and swallows his morning pills.

Today: a man who finds his sister's blown-off hand.
The picture in my head will drill there forever.

You don't know me, I say. *You have no idea who I am.*
My husband says, *Nobody knows anyone else.*

This response is not unloving.
He is a good man, a caring man.

I reheat my coffee before I walk the dog.
When we get back from the walk, the coffee is cold.

All day I reheat my same cup.

✳ November 8 ✳

Day after day, sip after sip, we piece together
our lives. I wanted to laugh at my student

who finished his memoir at nineteen, but wasn't he
right? Maybe everything significant happens

before you are seven. You pull a hangnail
and conceptualize pain. The grocery boy with the box

on the back of his bike brings the wrong order.
Cooked beans can't be uncooked. Time irreversible.

If you open one eye at a time, you can see
your own nose, how it sticks up into the air

like the lighthouse your grandfather took you to see
on the shore of Lake Michigan. You climbed

the tower into another world. So many worlds
there are. And are. The night you wept

because your brand new talking doll said only
five different things and couldn't answer questions.

We long for someone to tell us something real.

✳ November 9 ✳

I see you. I mean *you*. Or at least I imagine you,
reader, *lecteur*, someone with the kindness

to thumb through thirty pages of stitched scraps.
I want to know who *you* are. I want us to walk

in Forest Park, maybe along the Maple Trail,
while you tell me about your parents

or grandparents. What did you learn from them?
I learned manners and tragedy and also poetry.

And on a few happy summer evenings,
rum raisin ice cream. Can you still taste

your childhood? We need to tell each other
all these small details because after we're gone,

who'll care? In this life, I care about *you*.

Do you feel physically safe? Mostly I do.
Roofed. Fed. Insured. Unshot at by cops.

This might be my poem about being White.
Notice I can fit it neatly onto one page.

Sure, the wrong skin color in Kenya, in India,
but I was a privileged American tourist

with dollars, and therefore forgiven.
Back in the U.S. of A., in the various jobs

where I scrubbed or served, colorless,
people barely saw me. Or saw I was female.

Yes, I'll get you coffee. I'll hang up your coat.
I'll let you call me *the girl*. But I am someone.

Deep inside, under the pale skin you can see,
I am one of the sacred billions of animals

under the sun, the moon, the arched bridge
over the city river. I won't use words like *respect*.

My sermon: *See us. Each and every one.*

✳ November 11 ✳

What are the words stuck in your head?
Do they haunt you?

Mine do:
the eleventh hour of the eleventh day of the eleventh month

when they ended World War I in a railroad car on a siding.
I mean, where they signed the Armistice

that led to the Treaty of Versailles
that led to World War II.

Why was I taken there as a child
and why can't I stop remembering?

Maybe it's the very rhythm of the phrase:
the e-LEV-enth HOUR of the e-LEV-enth DAY of the e-LEV-enth
*   MONTH.*

Sometimes I think I am the surface of a lake
perturbed by every passing breeze that blows.

To Disturb. Turbulence. Perturb.
To modify the motion of a body by exerting a gravitational
*   force.*

So I am this body. So modified.

My favorite part of my body is my feet.
Do my feet show on this page?

Flexible. Mechanically functional. So symmetrical.
One smooth line from great toe to small.

And how often I walk out barefoot.
On wet leaves. Pebbles. Over snow to the mailbox.

Lava. Marsh. Sand. Pine needles. Shale.
Barefoot is how I go upon this earth—

a creature who walks back and forth upon the earth
or flies above it, knowing

the folds of the hills and green-belted tracks of its rivers,
Euphrates, Nile, Amazon, Ganges, Fifteen Mile Creek.

In some cave, hutch, yurt, raised hut over the flood,
we squatted with bare feet, pushed out our babies,

wove sandals, chatted about the neighbors, the stained
bottoms of our feet hardened like bark. How this world

pains us. Calloused might be easier.

✳ November 13 ✳

At three and a half I sat on the rug,
cross-legged and holding my new baby sister.

I remember white flannel. I don't remember
exclaiming *It moves!*

Last week I flew cross-country to visit her.
We toured a museum in her city.

Oh, that the dead could see — look, Mother,
your two girls together and at a museum.

So much, so little, we have in common.
You wouldn't think we had the same parents:

I with the harsh mother, she, the critical father.
We tell our grandchildren different stories.

What will anyone remember about me?
Does my sister know how I eat an apple?

The entire apple, core and all the seeds.

What do you know about apples?
Wikipedia: *A deciduous tree in the rose family*

best known for its sweet, pomaceous fruit,
the apple. The tree originated in Central Asia.

No, I mean useful knowledge. Good and Evil.
I was pulled over for eating an apple —

the officer thought I was on my cell phone.
Sinner, sinner, sink or swimmer. I wasn't.

This I know: Evil has nothing to do with sex.
Evil is just a failure of the imagination —

the failure to imagine the humanity of others,
the *me* of a mouse, the essential spirit in each tree.

Let's leave these windfall apples for the deer.

Animals. The non-human ones. They haunt me.
The dog Laika in her tiny Russian space capsule.

A stray plucked from the street. One of several.
Trained to stay still. Wear the equipment.

Chosen for how sweetly she tilted her head.
Pre-flight, one of the scientists took her home

to play with his kids. For years we were told
how she was euthanized — not that she fried.

After placing Laika in the container and before
closing the hatch, we kissed her nose, knowing

she would not survive. Laika, you still survive.
Nine orbits of the earth. Sixty years in my mind.

Sputnik 2 crossed above our yard. I waved.

After Sputnik we were all supposed to study math.
Now it's programming. I mean coding.

Study harder, kids. The world is getting ahead of you.
Great power, my ass. Watch out for China. Watch out

for all of 'em. When I was young I thought *U.S.*
stood for *us*, our red white and blue team

at the center of the world. Then I studied French.
Spanish. Portuguese. German. Latin.

I was meant to join the Foreign Service.
Achieve. Succeed. Instead I had babies:

small animals sucking at my full breasts.
For awhile it made sense. But only for awhile.

When my son learned to talk and never shut up,
I went back to school to hear adults speak. Or

did I know I'd need that academic union card?
M.A., Ph.D., give me a break. I say *Cursed be those*

who called me smart. Decades I was stupid.
Self-defeating. Working too hard. Playing

the wrong game. And the men in my life?
Not worth discussing. *For a smart girl,*

said my mom, *how can you be so dumb?*

✴ November 17 ✴

They taught us long division in May
and I forgot it over summer vacation.

When I learned it again in September
I carefully carried the remainder

as if in my arms—that poor little remainder,
too small and un-housed—until I could

bring a zero to keep it company.
I was that sad remainder struggling

to fit in, be part of the answer. Algebra
would feel so much less alien—

it used letters which were my friends.
Now when I swim laps I do arithmetic

in my head. The remainder swims with me
glued against my skin. Or I set it next to

the roses I prune, the man I love, recipes
I measure inaccurately, always knowing

how terrible it is to be left alone at the end.

Let's take a wider view. We are just modern
placental mammals, distantly descended from

small furry mammals who lived with dinosaurs.
Recently they found our oldest ancestor's teeth:

145 million years old. Nocturnal. Some of us
inherit that. I type too late at night

because there's so damn much I need to include:
my neighbor's cat who tiptoes the fence top,

local stars in the Milky Way, the *hoo* of owls,
the wild whip of Douglas firs, the puckered mouth

of a trout catching bugs—a circle on the flat pond.
You might ask if my writing has a plot. No, none,

or only that life is born and dies. Even rocks,
and I do believe they are *alive*, even the rocks

came into being and will wear away. No plot,
no mystery, no surprise. Nope, don't believe me.

It's all mystery, one continual surprise.

I was surprised at my first bumps of breasts.
I'd thought they would arrive complete, as if

two pockets in the ribs unzipped to pop them out.
Silliest was a *training* bra. Just what, I wondered,

did breasts get trained to do? I didn't understand
the tricks ahead: the sometimes firmness of nipples,

the mammalian mystery of milk, the greater mystery
of men's obsession. Don't misunderstand me:

I have perfectly good ones. They've performed
just fine. I nursed until my kids got top front teeth.

Afterwards nothing dangled like the teats
of a bitch dog. All these years, I've been glad

to be female, except for less salary and more
groping. I mean, talk about gross. Of course

I get mad, but why do I also feel pity?

So is gender the primary fact of our lives?
When I was young, I never suspected it.

Now when I walk in the woods, down any sidewalk,
I am a woman walking. Woman thinking.

Those men who choose to trans into women,
guys who think they were female all along,

what do they know of bleeding in sixth grade,
staining the panties, the skirt, the chair?

They were never embarrassed to buy Kotex.
They never explore inserting tampons.

They didn't have cramps in the nurse's office.
Do they know how to scrub out blood?

What I can't scrub out is Loehman's dressing room
where I first saw old ladies' undergarments:

girdles, boned corsets, garters pressing into flesh.
Would that be me if I ever got old? Yet sometimes

I can't distinguish: Is that an old woman? old man?

It's raining, it's pouring, the old man is snoring.
He went to bed, bumped his head, and couldn't

get up in the morning. Why didn't I sense
how sad that was? I happily recited it in rain,

pleased to have something pertinent to say.
I have loved old men, too many gone. For those

still here, let them not bump their white heads.
Let them kick off their quilts in the morning. Drink

coffee. Maybe check scores in the paper. Know
that someone needs them to linger

just for the deep sweetness in them. Way beyond
any sweetness a woman can muster.

No matter how old, women stay fierce.

Fierce when we need to be fierce.
Protect our kids from bullets. Find food for the pot.

Too often it's about money. Shoes outgrown
or no shoes at all. The rubber thong of the flip-flop

between street-stained toes. Or to pay a dentist.
Check the teeth: you see who grew up poor.

Me, I grew up privileged fake-poor. No Kleenex—
go blow your nose in toilet paper. No money for glue—

mix flour and water. My map project for school
turned out bumpy with lumps after I'd traced the map

with such exquisite care. Later my son would covet
Nike Air Jordans, a whole Con Ed electric bill.

Now I can splurge. Plane tickets. Theater tickets.
Despite the fear I'll outlive my money. Constantly

I study the homeless in doorways. Plan where
I'd string my shabby blue tarp. The truest truth:

I love my roof. I love my roof. I love my roof.

Thanksgiving, 2017. Shall I list my thanks?
For you, reading. My son at my sister's house.

For my daughter with old friends. For Mister
Turkey Carver. For you, still reading.

For the fact that nobody started a war today.
Alas, we've come to that. Dried teasels

in a crimson glass vase, and tall candles
to match. My Nana's silver. The dog

waiting to lick these gold-rimmed plates.
Late yellow trees. This flock of in-laws.

My mother's cranberry relish with oranges.
The smidgeon of rum in my mashed yams.

That this planet has a moon. My thumbs.
Our scarred table with nine boards. The roof again.

The same old stories about the same old cars.
The teasing, mostly. The pattern of cloud and sun

gilding the wall. Our English language.

I'm thankful for words, synonyms, shades
and options. Gradations of *joyous, happy,*

glad, cheerful, contented, unvexed. Nothing
I need on sale today. No shopping with mobs.

Turkey soup. Dog walks in the rain. Thinking
of Christmas. *Wouldn't let poor Rudolph*

join in any reindeer games. I was a misfit
for years. I wanted to be a brave pilot in China

flying the Hump. Heroic understatement
at twenty thousand feet. *He'll go down*

in his-story. What about *my* story? Maybe this
is what I do best: this mental striptease.

Not just for you. Also for my loving husband
so he'll understand why certain stories on NPR

make me cry. Music, yes, it's usually music,
makes him teary. Not the peculiar isolation

of even a long and happy marriage.

I write for a multiple audience: readers, of course,
but also my husband. And my children, grandson,

sister, dead parents and grandparents, friends, all
the kids in second grade, including smelly Billy.

I grew up on the #7 Broadway subway line
and in the Museum of Modern Art.

My mother took me to admire Monet's *Waterlilies*
and Picasso's spooky, mixed-up *Guernica*.

But starting when I was almost eight
I'd take myself to the bank of the Hudson

where the reeds were taller than I was
and whiskery hoboes smiled when I said *Hi*.

Nothing there scared me, not even big rats—
wild animals belonged in my wilderness.

I was an explorer and nobody else
had ever traversed these exact same rocks.

New Jersey was the beginning of the West
and from here I could almost swim there.

Now, decades later, I live in the far West
but my feet still smell of Hudson tidal mud

and I still hear Picasso's distorted horse screaming
under Fascist bombs, no matter how hard I've tried

to scuff my school shoes clean.

Women stitch. We don't start wars. Troy
wasn't Helen's idea. Blame Lust, the Gods.

Or some historians say Trade Routes.
But that would be Money, wouldn't it?

There's also Creed that differentiates the *us*
from the *them*. But so much more we share.

I need my girlfriends. A light knocking.
I leave off scribbling. Hurry to the door.

I could have told her *I'm busy*
but I don't. Instead I reheat breakfast coffee,

hear about her relatives at Thanksgiving,
the quilt she'll sell at the Christmas bazaar—

colors, pattern, backing. At last I dare confess
I'm stitching a November quilt out of words.

We hug before she goes.

We need to practice being wise together
while ice shelves crack into the sea. You

know the litany: Polar bears can't catch seals.
The rhinos are dying. Also monarchs.

Plant milkweed. Drive less. Mend. Send
garbage to China and let them send it back

transformed. Nothing makes sense.
And we were so well-intentioned.

Some being in another galaxy may tell
our story. Or not. And will that matter?

My dog knows how to live. She sniffs
the goodness of the earth, the shit

and carrion. She licks the crusted tears
at the corners of my sleepy eyes.

If I had a tail, I would wag it. Like this.

Give me a dog or a baby. Someone who loves
without complicated requirements. Sure, my parents

cared. My Nana. But everything was tied to being
a very good girl. And too many ways to be bad:

wrong face, tone of voice, arrangements of the hair.
Nobody told me: *Don't murder, Don't steal.*

It was all how to hold a fork. Late Victorian childhood
as ongoing guessing game. Often I guessed

wrong. Come high school I would like dissecting
frogs just for their lack of ambiguity. Pin it down

and name the parts correctly. Or learning French
to become someone else. How long it took

to be good enough. I can't fix the damaged world but
I pick up trash in the park. I joke with old people. I cook.

Lord, how I cook. Do you want to come to supper?

✳ November 29 ✳

There's this dream I dream. I've dreamt it for years.
I'm busy fixing supper for four when an extra person

shows up. I add a huge tomato to the salad. Doorbell:
two more. I boil rice. My neighbor stops over. I invite

her to stay. I quick microwave frozen spinach.
Serve it with grated cheese and grace. How easy

I make it look. Superwoman. Never the researcher
curing cancer. Not some pilot whose perilous mission

may save the world. Just a woman in a kitchen.
I suspect a moral here but what is it?

I have a sister forty thousand years old. She kneels
by a fire at the mouth of a cave. Her hair is sooty.

She raises her head to look at me. We both grin.

✳ November 30 ✳

Thanks for reading to the end. I didn't expect you
to stay. Well, we've run out of days. Nothing

I've told you isn't true. I wish I knew more about
you. My cell phone is 503-819-0975. Really.

Call and tell me who you are. I promise to listen.
I'm totally safe to talk to. Not a pervert or scammer.

Of course I might write about you someday,
but I wouldn't use your name without permission.

My husband, I warned him before we got married,
and my kids, my sister, my parents were fair game.

A dog doesn't care what we write. I write about dogs
incessantly. I know I'm another breathing animal

on a planet in a solar system in a galaxy spinning
through eons. No non-human animal contemplates

deep time. But you have. That's part of why
I love you so much. You've been a good friend

all month, and I'll miss you. Happy December.
And if I never stitch another quilt, so be it.

Please don't hang this one on a wall or store it
safe from moths in a zippered plastic bag.

Spread this quilt to keep another reader warm.

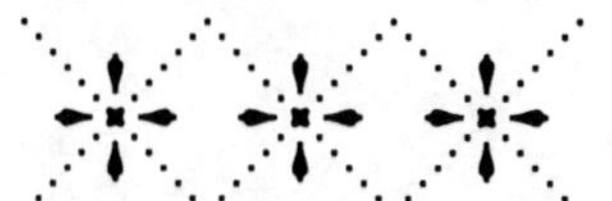

Praise for
November Quilt

"Penelope Scambly Schott's award-winning chapbook of thirty poems—organized and titled as one-a-day offerings for the month of November—reads like a series of brief, conversational letters to the reader. Longings are shared, intimacies revealed, disappointments confessed. Along the way, truths are discovered and delivered aphoristically: 'Lives don't have plots; they have refrains.' Thoughtful and thought-provoking, these poems are not as much meditations as they are invitations—to ponder, to converse, to be disturbed, to love, to never forget. 'Sometimes,' Schott writes, 'I am the surface of a lake / perturbed by every passing breeze that blows.' In *November Quilt*, she blows back."

~ Andrea Hollander,
author of *Blue Mistaken for Sky*

About the Author

Penelope Scambly Schott leads a double life. In Portland, Oregon she goes to theater and poetry events and she and her husband host the White Dog Poetry Salon in their home on a hill. In Dufur, Oregon (population 604) she and the white dog climb D hill between the wheat fields and admire the east side of Mount Hood. Also in Dufur she writes and leads an annual poetry workshop. Here she and the dog wander about in the dark. The dog admires the dirt underpaw while the woman sniffs stars.

Penelope's verse biography *A is for Anne: Mistress Hutchinson Disturbs the Commonwealth* received an Oregon Book Award for Poetry. Other books include *Serpent Love: A Mother-Daughter Epic* about a struggle with her adult daughter, along with an essay in which the daughter gives her point of view, and *Bailing the River*, a poetry collection full of dogs, coyotes, and the unsolvable and sometimes funny mysteries of the ordinary. Most recent is *House of the Cardamom Seed*.

She is grateful to her family and her weekly hiking group as well as Word Sisters, Cool Women Poets of New Jersey, Pearls, and her far-flung on-line critique group.

About The Poetry Box®
Chapbook Prize

In 2018, The Poetry Box introduced their annual Chapbook Prize competition, awarding publication to at least one poet. The contest is open to both established poets and emerging talent alike, and the editors reserve the right to select more than one poet's manuscript for publication. Currently, the contest is open to poets residing in the United States and is open for submissions each year during the month of February.

2018 Winners:

First Prize:
Shrinking Bones by Judy K. Mosher (NM)

Second Prize:
November Quilt by Penelope Scambly Schott (OR)

Third Prize (tie):
14: Antología del Sonoran by Christopher Bogart (NJ)
Fireweed by Gudrun Bortman (CA)